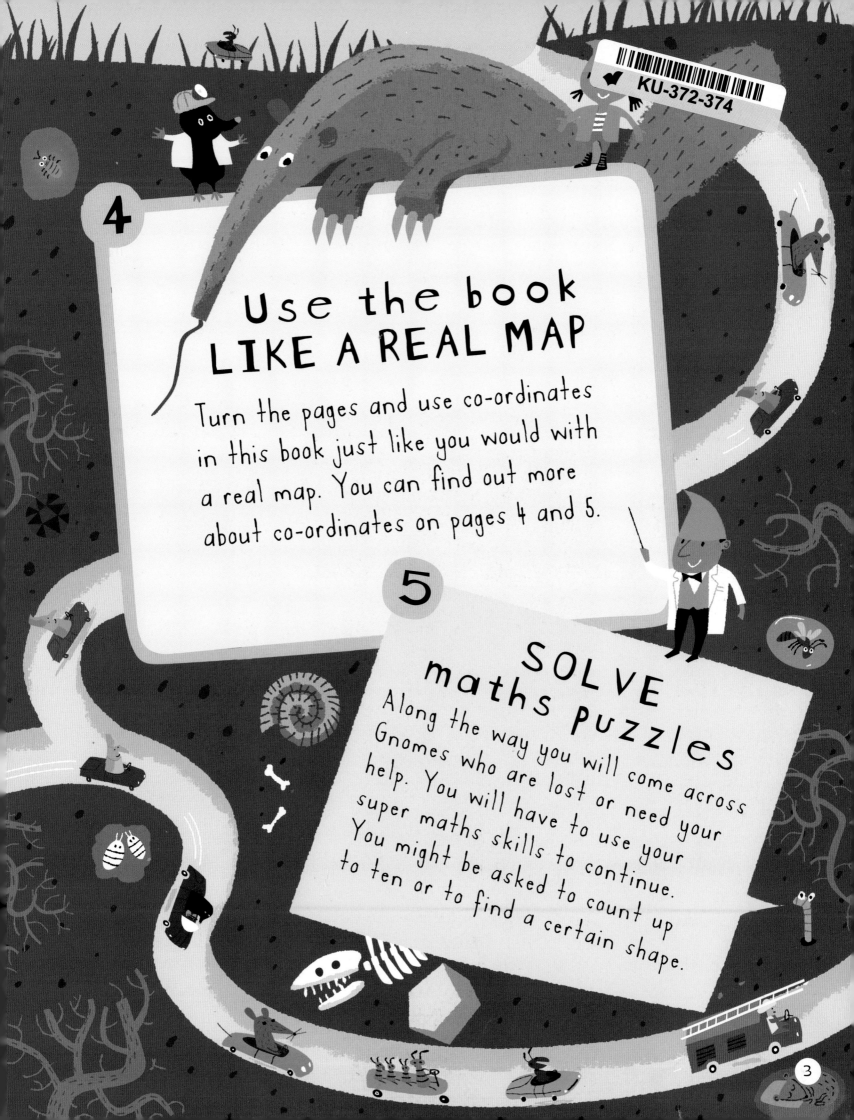

**4**

# Use the book LIKE A REAL MAP

Turn the pages and use co-ordinates in this book just like you would with a real map. You can find out more about co-ordinates on pages 4 and 5.

**5**

# SOLVE maths puzzles

Along the way you will come across Gnomes who are lost or need your help. You will have to use your super maths skills to continue. You might be asked to count up to ten or to find a certain shape.

# Welcome to Gnome City

Look at the map of Gnome City. Can you see where Luna's lair is?
It looks like a castle. That's where you need to get to. Let's use
co-ordinates to help us describe where Luna's lair is on the map.

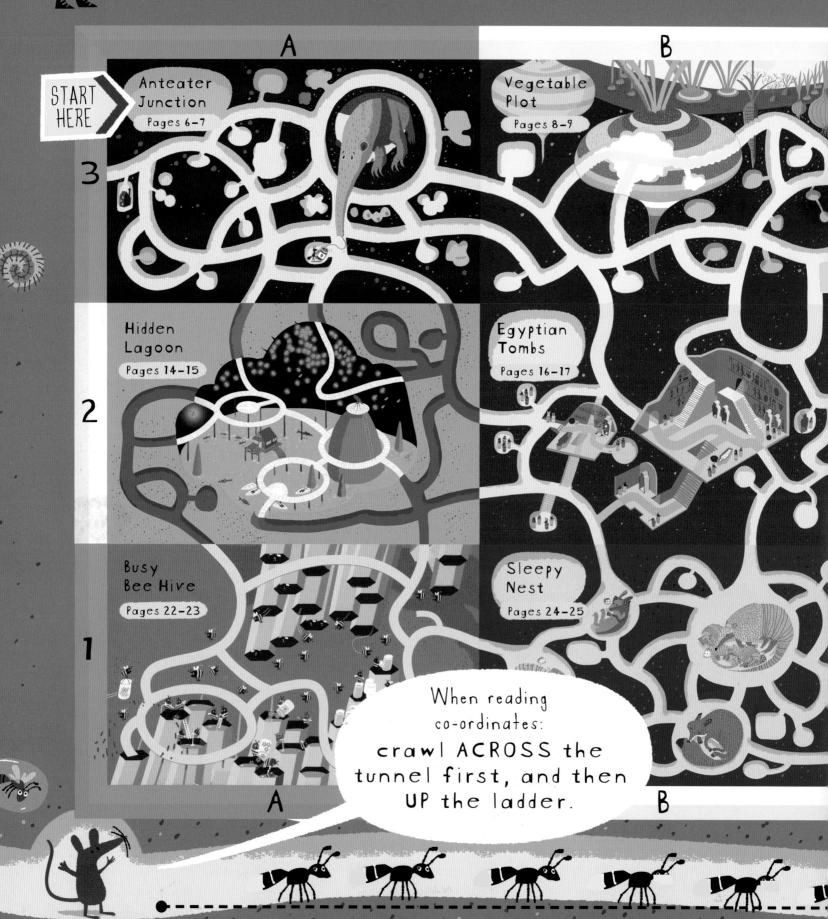

START HERE

**A**

**B**

3

Anteater
Junction
Pages 6–7

Vegetable
Plot
Pages 8–9

2

Hidden
Lagoon
Pages 14–15

Egyptian
Tombs
Pages 16–17

1

Busy
Bee Hive
Pages 22–23

Sleepy
Nest
Pages 24–25

**A**

**B**

When reading
co-ordinates:
**crawl ACROSS the
tunnel first, and then
UP the ladder.**

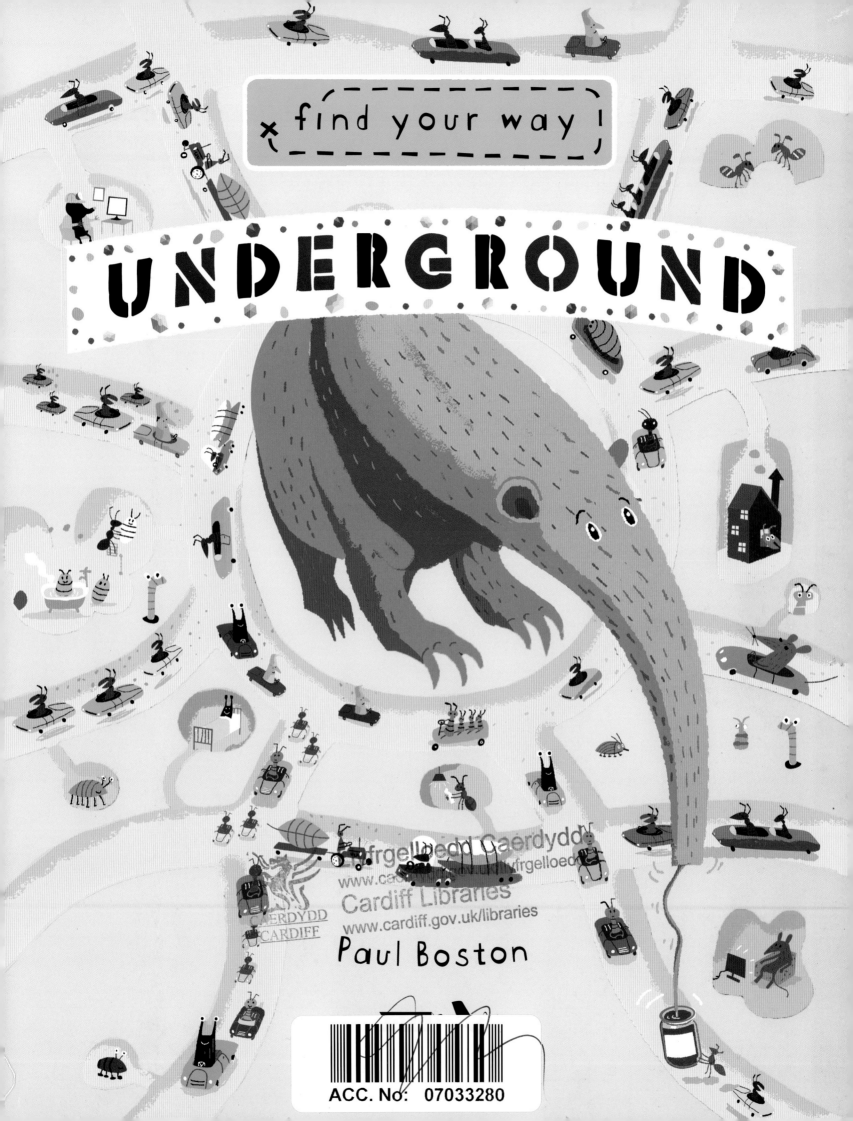

find your way

# UNDERGROUND

## Paul Boston

# YOUR MISSION

Us Gnomes are in trouble!
Luna the dragon has stolen our gold.
Are you brave enough to help us get it back?
Find your way to Luna's lair by choosing which
exits or entrances to follow on each page.

## 1 Choose your transport

Wagon

Frog

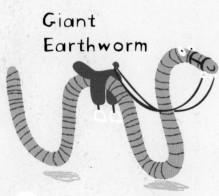
Giant Earthworm

## 2 Trace a route

There are lots to choose from and you can go BACKWARDS and FORWARDS along the same tunnel.

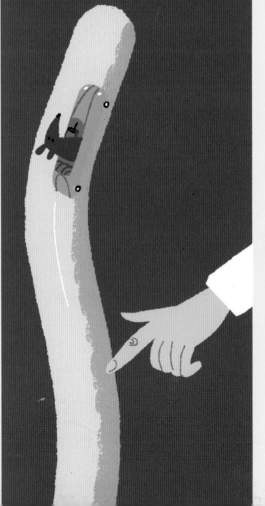

## 3 Collect on every page

Choose ONE of the missions below to help the Gnomes. You will find one of each object in every scene.

Collect 12 BUCKETS OF WATER to put out Luna's fires.

Collect 12 WHEELBARROWS to pick up all the gold.

Collect 12 MAGIC FLUTES to play a special tune that will send Luna off to sleep.

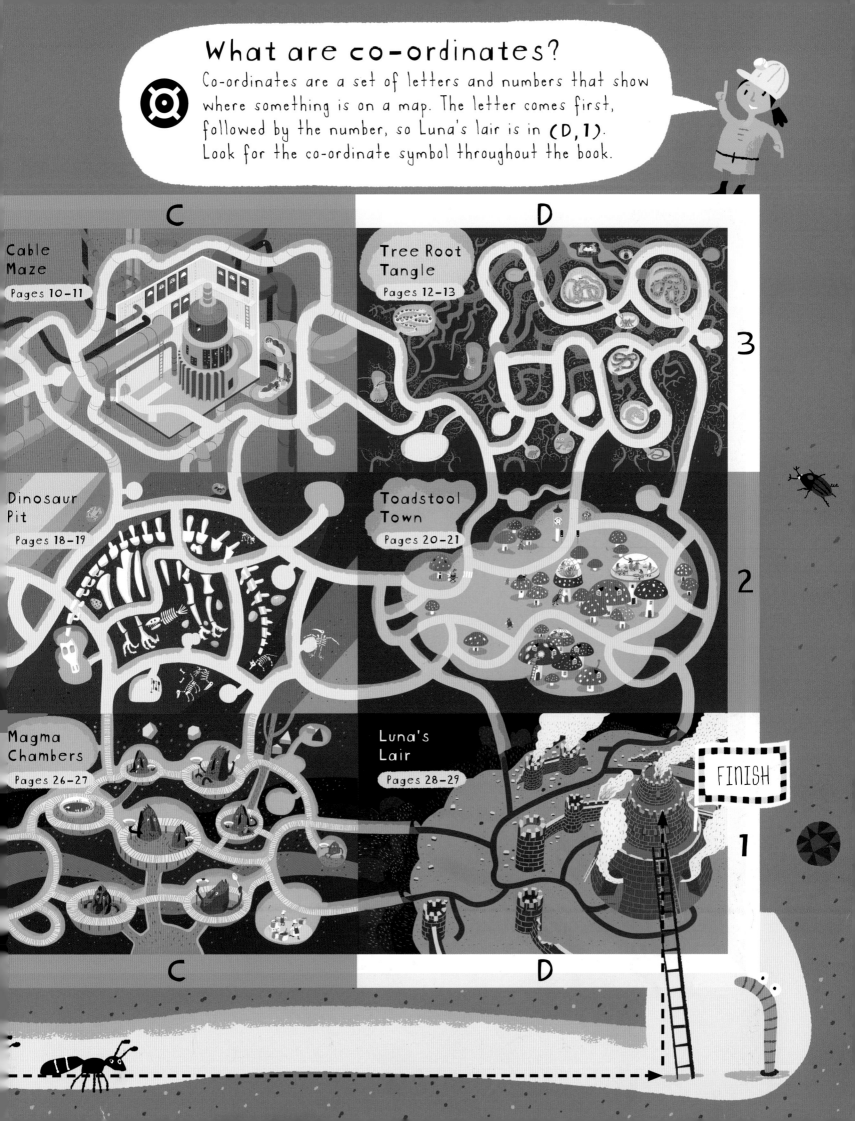

## What are co-ordinates?

Co-ordinates are a set of letters and numbers that show where something is on a map. The letter comes first, followed by the number, so Luna's lair is in (D,1). Look for the co-ordinate symbol throughout the book.

**C**

**D**

**Cable Maze**
Pages 10–11

**Tree Root Tangle**
Pages 12–13

**3**

**Dinosaur Pit**
Pages 18–19

**Toadstool Town**
Pages 20–21

**2**

**Magma Chambers**
Pages 26–27

**Luna's Lair**
Pages 28–29

FINISH

**1**

**C**

**D**

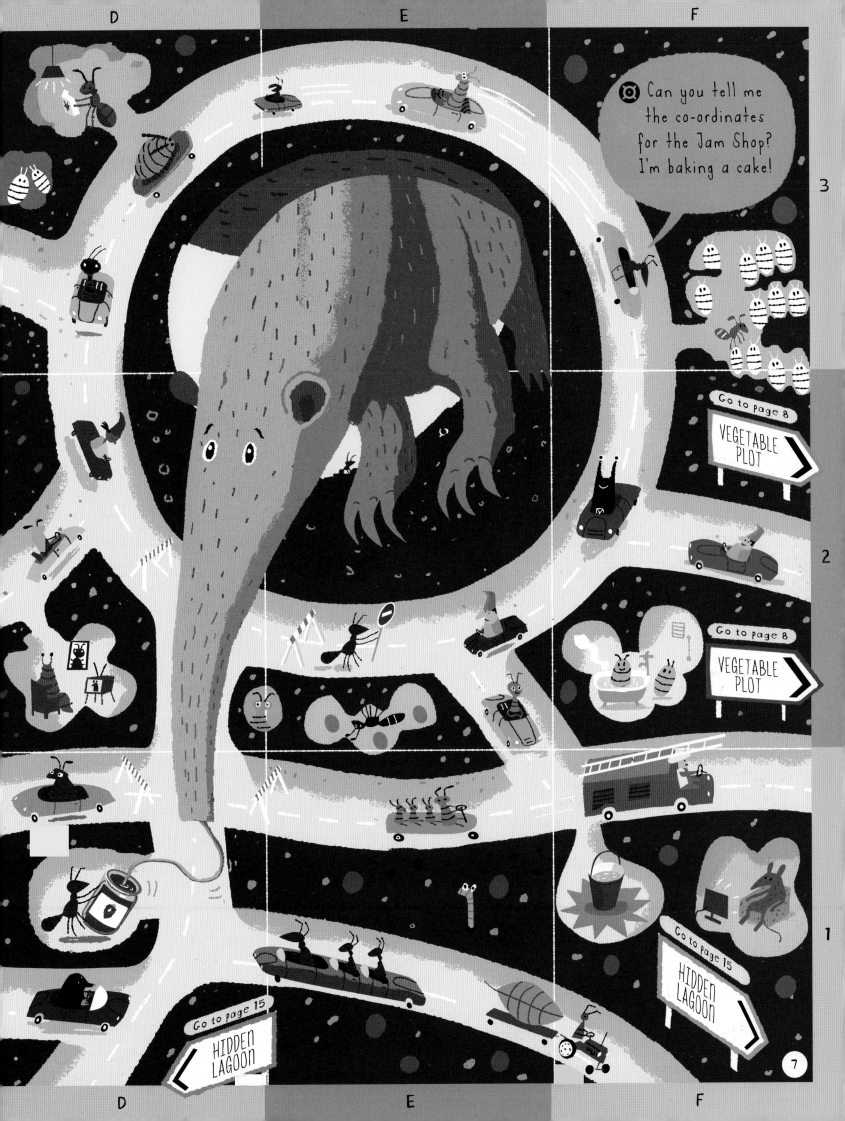

You've reached Cable Maze! This is where all the electricity and water comes from to deliver power to the Gnomes' homes. Stick to the path so you don't get lost.

BUCKET OF WATER

WHEELBARROW

MAGIC FLUTE

Go to page 9
VEGETABLE PLOT

Go to page 9
VEGETABLE PLOT

CABLE MAZE

Which naughty animal has climbed to the top of the power station?

Go to page 18
DINOSAUR PIT

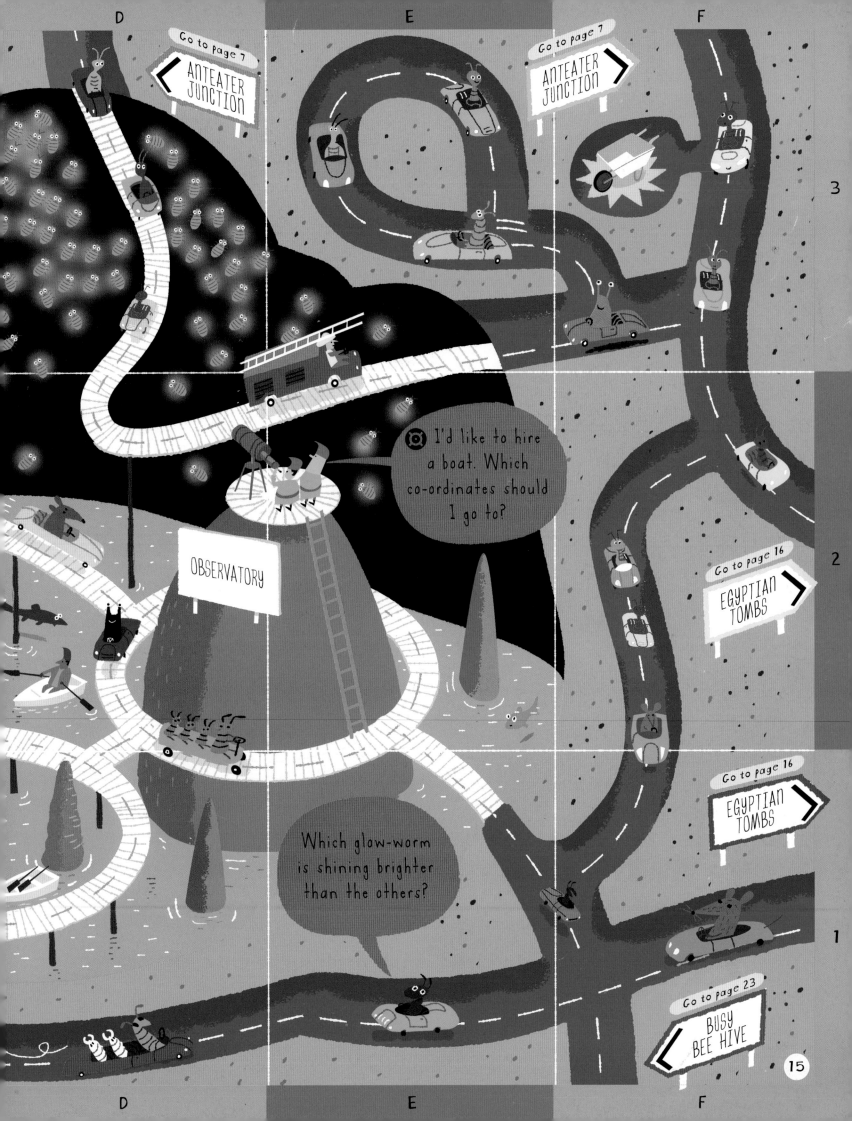

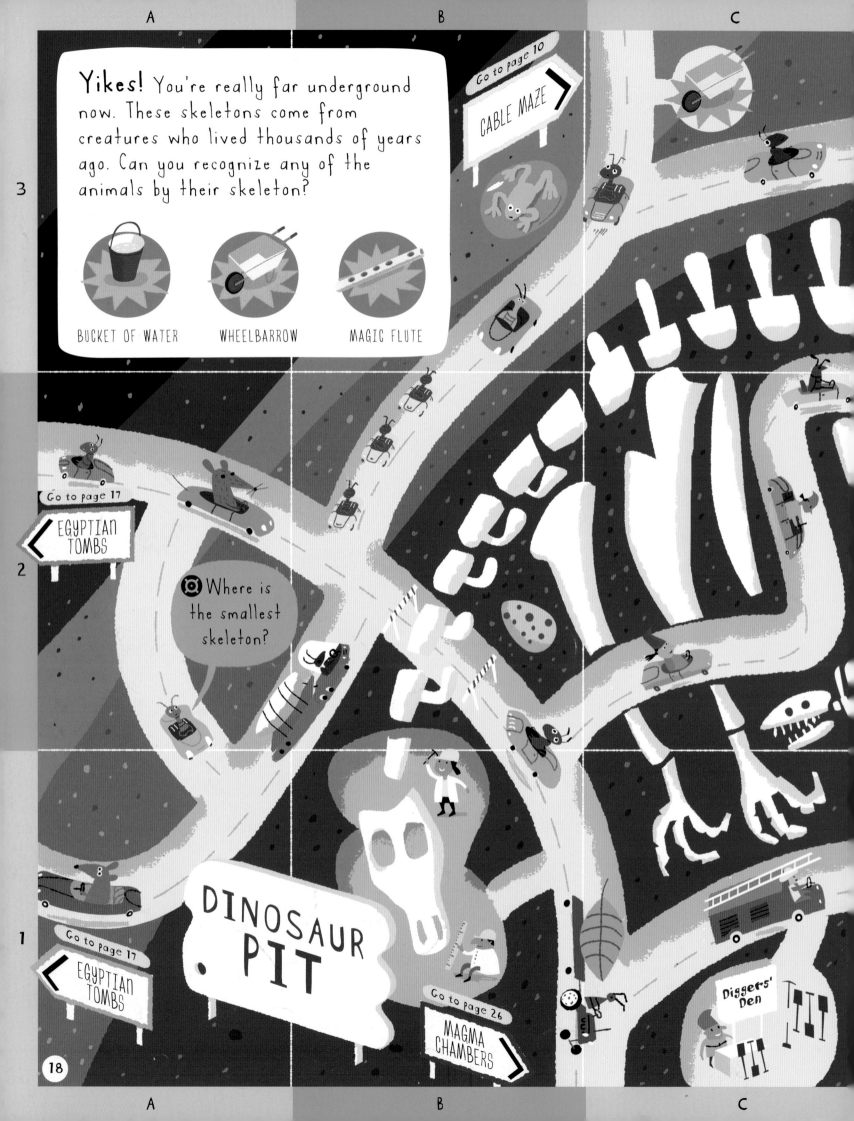

Yikes! You're really far underground now. These skeletons come from creatures who lived thousands of years ago. Can you recognize any of the animals by their skeleton?

BUCKET OF WATER

WHEELBARROW

MAGIC FLUTE

Go to page 10
CABLE MAZE

Go to page 17
EGYPTIAN TOMBS

Where is the smallest skeleton?

DINOSAUR PIT

Go to page 17
EGYPTIAN TOMBS

Go to page 26
MAGMA CHAMBERS

Diggers' Den

18

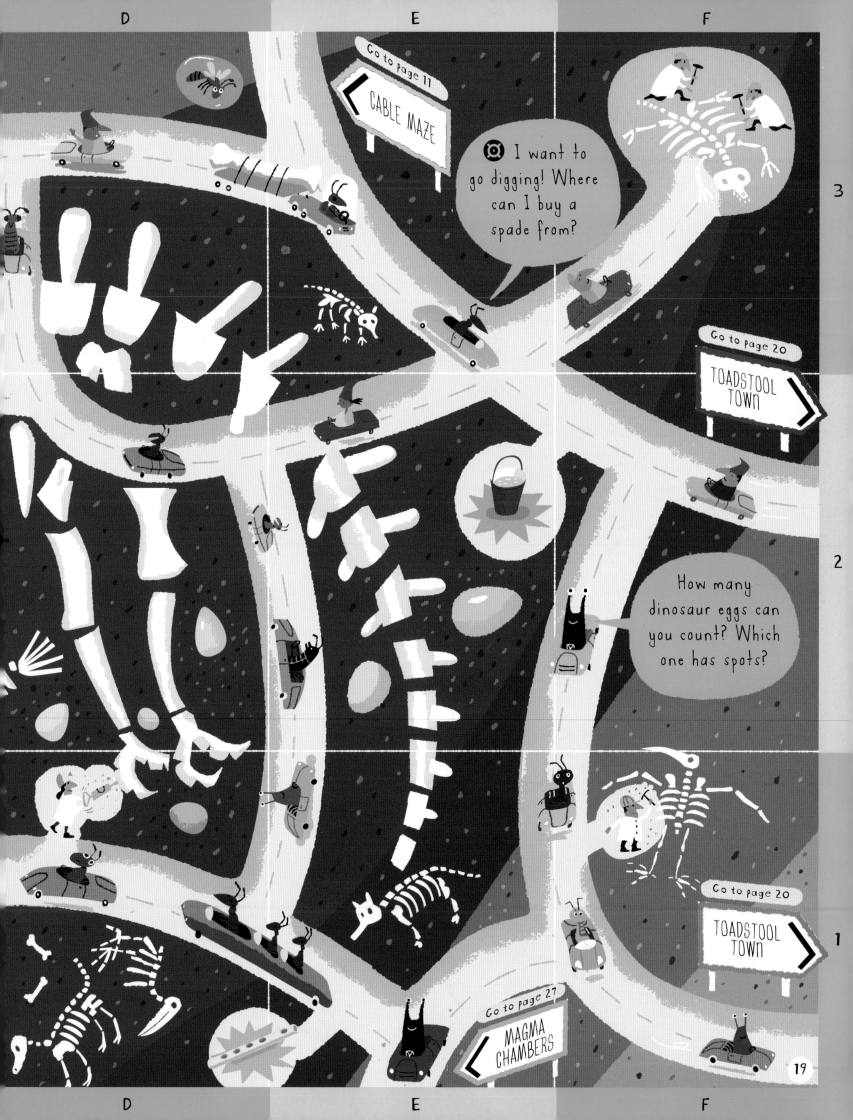

Bzzz, bzzz! Can you hear those busy bees? They're working really hard down here to make honey for the Gnomes. Can you see the Queen Bee? She's much bigger than the others!

BUCKET OF WATER

WHEELBARROW

MAGIC FLUTE

Go to page 14
HIDDEN LAGOON

22

# MORE FUN UNDERGROUND!

## Understanding Co-ordinates

Encourage your child to look at other places where they might find co-ordinates, such as on an A-Z map. Draw an underground map together and plan your route to the buried treasure.

## Counting

Go back through the book and look for more opportunities to encourage counting underground. How many legs does a beetle have? How many bees are making honey?

## Telling the Time

Together with your child, draw pictures of their daily routine and cut them out. These could include: waking up, having breakfast, going to school, having dinner and going to bed. Jumble up the pieces and ask them to put them in the correct order. Use a clock to discuss with your child at which time they carry out each activity. Talk about nocturnal creatures and the differences in their routine.

## Recognising Shapes

Use cardboard boxes and tubes to encourage underground small world play. Explain the boxes and tubes are similar to burrows and tunnels underground. Use the names of 3D shapes to describe the tunnels and burrows, e.g. cube, cylinder.

## Maths Problems and Vocabulary

Look for opportunities to build on mathematic vocabulary and problem solving skills. For example, if there are five Gnomes holding two buckets of water each, how many buckets are there altogether? Try to spot preposition vocabulary such as 'above', 'below', or 'under'.

## Measurements

Use a magnifying glass and explore the outside. What can you see hiding in the soil? Can you find a long worm? How about a small ant? Guess how many centimetres you think each one is.

**Q** Quarto Knows

Quarto is the authority on a wide range of topics.
Quarto educates, entertains and enriches the lives of our readers—enthusiasts and lovers of hands-on living.
www.quartoknows.com

Written and edited by: Joanna McInerney and the QED team
Designer: Mike Henson
Consultant: Alistair Bryce-Clegg

2016 © Quarto Publishing plc

This edition first published in paperback in 2018 by QED Publishing, an imprint of The Quarto Group.

The Old Brewery, 6 Blundell Street, London N7 9BH, United Kingdom.
T (0)20 7700 6700 F (0)20 7700 8066
www.QuartoKnows.com

A catalogue record for this book is available from the British Library.

ISBN 978 1 78603 287 4

Manufactured in Guangdong, China TT042018

9 8 7 6 5 4 3 2 1